MAKING MOVIES

Movie Animation

by Geoffrey M. Horn

J791.4
HOR

GARETH**STEVENS**
PUBLISHING
A Member of the WRC Media Family of Companies

Please visit our Web site at: www.garethstevens.com
For a free color catalog describing Gareth Stevens Publishing's
list of high-quality books and multimedia programs, call
1-800-542-2595 (USA) or 1-800-387-3178 (Canada).
Gareth Stevens Publishing's fax: (414) 332-3567.

Library of Congress Cataloging-in-Publication Data

Horn, Geoffrey M.
    Movie animation / by Geoffrey M. Horn.
      p. cm. — (Making movies)
    Includes bibliographical references and index.
    ISBN-10: 0-8368-6837-4 — ISBN-13: 978-0-8368-6837-1 (lib. bdg.)
    1. Animated films—Juvenile literature. I. Title.
  II. Series: Horn, Geoffrey M. Making movies.
  NC1765.H67   2007
  791.43'34—dc22   2006006746

This edition first published in 2007 by
Gareth Stevens Publishing
A Member of the WRC Media Family of Companies
330 West Olive Street, Suite 100
Milwaukee, WI 53212 USA

Concept: Sophia Olton-Weber
Managing Editor: Valerie J. Weber
Art direction and design: Tammy West
Picture research: Diane Laska-Swanke

Photo credits: Cover, Photofest; p. 5 © 20th Century Fox Film Corp./
Everett Collection; p. 7 © Alexander Caminada/Rex Features, courtesy
Everett Collection; p. 9 BBC Films/Photofest; pp. 11, 13, 18, 20
© Walt Disney/courtesy Everett Collection; p. 12 Walt Disney/Photofest;
pp. 16, 19 Walt Disney Pictures/Photofest; p. 22 New Line/Photofest;
pp. 24, 25 Lucasfilm Ltd./Photofest; pp. 28, 29 Studio Ghibli/Disney/Photofest

Printed in the United States of America

1 2 3 4 5 6 7 8 9 10 09 08 07 06

Contents

Cover: A scene from *Shrek* 2, which set box-office records in 2004.

CHAPTER 1

What Is Animation?

Welcome to a world where toys talk. Elephants fly. Donkeys tell jokes. Dogs read newspapers. Turtles chill out like surfer dudes. And a character can fall from a fifty-story building and walk away without a scratch.

This is the wild, wacky world of animation. The usual rules don't apply here. Animators are happy to suspend the laws of nature to tell a good story or get a big laugh.

Fooling the Eye

Animation comes from the Latin word *anima*. The word means "spirit," "breath," or "life." Animators make drawings, paintings, paper cutouts, clay puppets, or computer images appear to come alive. Methods differ. But all animators find ways to fool the human eye.

Here's how animation works. Imagine a series of sixteen pictures. They each show a slightly different face as it changes from a frown to a smile. Look at them one by one. They seem to be sixteen separate images. But if you flip through them very fast, your eyes will see them as a single moving image. This effect is called "persistence of vision."

All movies rely on persistence of vision. Movie film consists of many separate photos, or frames. A two-hour movie has more than 172,000 frames. But the human eye sees the whole film as a single moving picture.

Stop-Motion Animation

If you make a short movie of your dog, your camera

Director Chris Wedge checks sketches for his animated movie *Ice Age.*

5

What's the best way to get started in cartoons? Draw, draw — then draw some more. Draw pictures of your friends and family. Imitate the different styles you see in movies and on TV. Invent your own cartoon characters. Try telling a story through a series of drawings.

Take as many art classes as you can. Nearly all colleges offer courses in fine art. The California Institute of the Arts has a world-famous program in animation.

shoots hundreds of frames. As your dog moves, the camera records the motion at twenty-four frames per second. The camera does most of the work for you.

For animators, making things move is much harder. Some artists use computers to ease their task. For example, a computer program can change, or "morph," one image into a different image. Other artists imitate motion the old-fashioned way — frame by frame. Using this method, Nick Park and his staff made *Chicken Run*.

Park works for Aardman Animation. He is also the creator of Wallace and Gromit. Wallace is an inventor. Sometimes his ideas work. More often they go haywire. Gromit is Wallace's loyal dog. He is as sensible as Wallace is careless. Gromit never speaks. But movements of his eyes, brows, and ears tell us what he's thinking.

Park uses a method called stop-motion animation. (This method is sometimes known as Claymation.) Park and his aides work with clay puppets. They break down every puppet action into tiny movements. The artists adjust the puppets for each frame. They also tweak the sets and lighting. After each shot is taken, the separate frames are linked to make a sequence. The whole process takes a long time. The studio can make only about two minutes of film each week.

Each scene in a Wallace and Gromit movie uses miniature sets and puppets.

Behind the Scenes:
Making a Flipbook

A good way to try your hand at cartoons is to make a flipbook.

• Take a small pack of two- or three-hole notebook paper. Run a string or shoelace through the holes on one side. Tie the sheets together.

• Start with the last page. Make a pencil drawing near the edge of the page. For example, you might show someone dancing. The first sketch could show the dancer's feet close together.

• Turn to the next-to-last page. Redraw the same image but with a slight change. (You can trace most of the first image onto the new page.) For example, the left foot might now be slightly ahead of the right.

• Repeat these steps for a few pages. Then you can flip quickly through these pages to check your work; your drawing should appear to move.

• After you've drawn all the pages, flip through the book again. Make sure the action looks convincing. Change your drawings if it doesn't. Then add colors and background to give your flipbook a finished look.

Stop-motion is one of the oldest animation methods. But in Park's hands, the results still feel funny and fresh. In 2005, he came out with his first feature-length Wallace and Gromit movie — *The Curse of the Were-Rabbit*. In this film, Wallace hatches a harebrained scheme to keep rabbits out of vegetable gardens. As usual, the plan goes wrong, and Gromit saves the day. The movie won an Oscar for best animated film.

Director Tim Burton also has a fresh take on stop-motion. He used stop-motion in his weird tale *The Nightmare Before Christmas*. Burton used the same method in *Corpse Bride*, another eerie animated story.

CELEBRITY SNAPSHOT
Nick Park

Born: December 6, 1958, in Preston, Lancashire, Great Britain

Film Career: Animator, director, writer

Academy Awards: Winner for directing *Creature Comforts* (1990), *The Wrong Trousers* (1993), *A Close Shave* (1995), and *Wallace & Gromit in The Curse of the Were-Rabbit*

Other Top Films: *A Grand Day with Wallace & Gromit; Chicken Run*

Backstory: Nick Park made his first animated film when he was thirteen years old. He used puppets and the family movie camera. British TV aired one of his movies when he was seventeen. Many Americans first saw his work in a 1986 music video. The video was for "Sledgehammer," a hit song by Peter Gabriel.

Nick Park does animation the old-fashioned way — with handmade clay puppets.

CHAPTER 2

The Mouse That Roared

About one hundred years ago, Winsor McCay was a top cartoonist in New York City. His most popular cartoon strip was *Little Nemo*. This beautifully drawn strip ran in Sunday newspapers in color. Sometime around 1907, McCay had a bright idea. He decided to turn *Nemo* into a short cartoon film. He worked on the project for four years. In 1911, his hand-drawn cartoon was shown in a movie theater for the first time.

Gertie the Dinosaur

Little Nemo delighted audiences. But the McCay cartoon that really opened their eyes was *Gertie the Dinosaur*. This 1914 film used ten thousand separate drawings. McCay drew Gertie. An assistant drew all the backgrounds.

Gertie is filled with witty touches. But the most groundbreaking part of the film is Gertie herself. She is big and strong enough to eat a tree. But she is sensitive enough to cry when she is scolded.

Ever since McCay's Gertie, animals have been cartoon favorites. Bugs Bunny, Garfield, Snoopy — these creatures have all become cartoon superstars. But the biggest star of all was one of the smallest — a mouse named Mickey.

The Magic of Disney

Mickey Mouse made Walt Disney famous. Disney learned the basics of cartoon art in the early 1920s. In 1922, he began working with an artist friend, Ub Iwerks. They started the Laugh-o-Gram studio in Kansas City. A year later, Disney moved to Hollywood. There, Walt and his brother Roy formed Disney Productions. Iwerks soon headed west to join them.

Together they turned the cartoon world upside down. Until the late 1920s, cartoons had no soundtracks.

Mickey Mouse was the first cartoon character to become an international superstar.

Walt Disney

Born: December 5, 1901, in Chicago, Illinois

Died: December 15, 1966, in Burbank, California

Film Career: Producer, director, animator

Academy Awards: Won twenty-six Oscars, including special awards for creating *Mickey Mouse*, producing *Snow White and the Seven Dwarfs* (1937), and making *Fantasia* (1940)

Backstory: One of Disney's early cartoons showed Oswald the Lucky Rabbit. The Disney company found creative ways to make money from Oswald. It encouraged the sale of Oswald-related products. For example, it collected money from a company that wanted to make Oswald the Lucky Rabbit candy bars. Disney later earned money from thousands of items based on Mickey Mouse and other cartoon figures.

Walt Disney studies models for *Snow White and the Seven Dwarfs*.

Snow White's music as well as its animation charmed audiences. It was nominated for an Oscar for music.

Live performers provided the sound. Often, a piano would play while the movie was showing. Walt Disney changed all that. In 1928, he made *Steamboat Willie*. This Mickey Mouse cartoon came with its own soundtrack. The music and sound effects were perfectly timed to match the on-screen action.

Expanding the Art

Disney kept cranking out Mickey Mouse cartoons for an eager public. But he also continued to push the frontiers of film art. In 1932, the Disney team made the first full-color cartoon, *Flowers and Trees*. Disney's first feature-length cartoon, *Snow White and the Seven*

Behind the Scenes:
The Disney Empire

The Walt Disney Company still makes cartoons. But the firm has many other ways to make money. Disney owns Disneyland in California and Walt Disney World and Epcot in Florida. Overseas, Disney partly owns theme parks in Europe and Asia. Among Disney's TV holdings are ABC, ESPN, and the Disney Channel. The company even runs its own cruise line. In 2005, the Disney empire made a profit of about $2.5 billion.

Dwarfs, came five years later.

The risks were high. Making *Snow White* cost more than $1 million — a huge sum in those days. Would the public sit still for a full-length cartoon? No one knew until Disney made one. Audiences were amazed that a cartoon could be so powerful. People expected a cartoon to make them laugh. They didn't expect a cartoon to frighten them — or move them to tears.

In 1940, Disney tried another risky idea. *Fantasia* (fan-TAY-zha) was a full-length cartoon based on classical music. Each piece of music was matched to a different drawing style. Mickey Mouse appeared in *Fantasia*. So did dinosaurs and waltzing hippos. Some segments were funny. Others were delicate. One part was very violent. *Fantasia* proved that a cartoon could be great art.

Computer Animation

CHAPTER 3

For seventy years, the basic tools
of cartooning remained the same.
The artist might start with drawings
or paintings or paper cutouts or clay.
But everything needed to be put on film
frame by individual frame. This was —
and still is — very costly.

One way of cutting costs was to cheapen
the product. During the 1950s, the market
for full-length cartoons began to dry up. But
TV had a huge appetite for shorter cartoons
for series. Animation for the small screen could
be simpler and cruder. The stories changed.
The scripts varied. But many of the character
movements and backgrounds were repeated,
helping the studios cut costs. By the 1970s, it
looked like animation had reached a dead end.

Tron

In 1982, the Disney studio released a new kind
of animated feature — *Tron*. In *Tron*, Jeff Bridges

plays a designer of computer games. His ideas are being ripped off. While tracking down the thief, Bridges enters the computer world he helped create.

Animators used computers to produce some scenes in *Tron*. Other scenes mix live action with backgrounds made by computers. The filmmakers called their method "painting with light."

Tron did not do very well at the box office or with critics. Much of *Tron* felt more like a video game than a movie. Still, *Tron* was an important film. It challenged artists to explore what computers could do. The founders of Pixar Animation Studio took up that challenge — with spectacular success.

The Pixar Story
Two men had key roles in the birth of Pixar. The first was John Lasseter. Before coming to Pixar, he

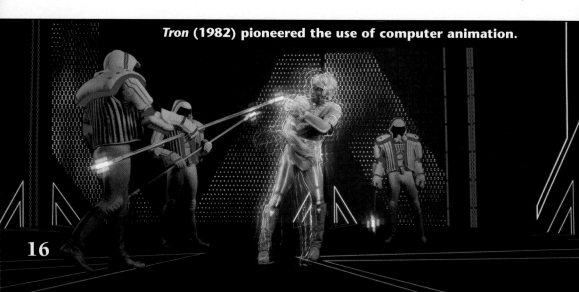

Tron (1982) pioneered the use of computer animation.

worked for Disney. He also did special effects for George Lucas, the maker of *Star Wars*. Another key figure in Pixar was Steve Jobs. Jobs was a founder of Apple Computer — and a very rich man. He paid $10 million to set up Pixar in 1986.

Pixar didn't start out as a movie studio. Its first business was computer systems. These systems were very good at creating and displaying images. To

show what the systems could do, Lasseter began making short films. Lasseter's short cartoons were so good that Pixar decided to try a feature-length film. Released in 1995, *Toy Story* was the first full-length cartoon made completely by computer.

Toy Story was a perfect marriage of old and new. Lasseter started with a great cast of characters — toys in a playroom. Many of the toys had an old-fashioned look, like Mr. Potato Head and Woody the cowboy. The script

17

CELEBRITY SNAPSHOT
John Lasseter

Born: January 12, 1957, in Hollywood, California

Film Career: Animator, director, producer, writer

Academy Awards: For directing *Tin Toy* (1988); special award for leading Pixar's *Toy Story* team (1995)

Other Top Films: *A Bug's Life*; *Toy Story 2*; *Cars*

Backstory: Lasseter says *Cars* (2006) is a film he was born to direct. While making *Cars*, he visited auto factories and racing shops. He also took race-car driving lessons. "All this is called research," he says. "But it's a whole lot of fun for me." He tells directors to choose their subjects wisely. "If it's something you truly love, it is like playing the whole time."

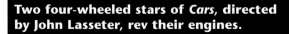

Two four-wheeled stars of *Cars*, directed by John Lasseter, rev their engines.

Toy Story **soared, thanks to Pixar's animated heroes Buzz Lightyear and Woody.**

was fun. The dialogue was crisp. The music was delightful. Unlike *Tron*, the art in *Toy Story* didn't look like a computer did it. It looked real.

In later films, Pixar continued to break new ground. For example, Pixar took great care in creating Sulley, a shaggy monster in *Monsters, Inc.* Sulley's coat had 3.2 million hairs. Every time Sulley

For many years, males controlled the cartoon industry. For example, the founders of the Disney company were men. So were the founders of Pixar. Some women held low-paying jobs in animation studios. But few got the chance to make their own cartoons.

Faith Hubley was an exception. She made cartoons with her husband, John. Together they were nominated for six Oscars and won two. She continued to make cartoons after he died in 1977.

Since the early 1990s, many more women have entered the cartoon field. Animator and teacher Michelle Meeker thinks good things will come of the change. "Women know how women move," she says. "Men think they know. But usually they don't."

moved, the computer could control each hair separately. The technical skill was amazing. But Pixar didn't use this high-tech stuff just to show off. Pixar used computers to tell a good story amazingly well.

With *The Incredibles*, Pixar's artists continued to stretch their skills.

Between Two Worlds

In a bloody scene in *Lord of the Rings*, Gollum and Frodo struggle for the ring of power. Gollum bites Frodo's hand and grabs the ring. But before Gollum can put on the ring, Frodo lunges at him. Both Frodo and Gollum tumble over a ledge. Frodo hangs on until his friend Sam can rescue him. Gollum, still clutching the precious ring, falls into a lake of fire.

Frodo is a real actor. Gollum is animated. The scene is so well done, you can hardly tell the difference.

Blurring the Boundaries

From the beginning, some cartoon artists have blurred the line between what's real and what's not. For example, Winsor McKay used *Gertie the Dinosaur* in a stage show. At the end of the show, he made it look like he was stepping from the stage into the movie. The "movie McKay" got on

Gertie's back, and the two rode off together. The audience loved it.

Walt Disney's early movies also blended real people with fantasy. His *Alice Comedies* in the 1920s were based on *Alice in Wonderland*. In these short films, a four-year-old girl plays Alice. Cartoon characters enter Alice's world. Alice also pays a visit to Cartoonland.

From Mary Poppins to Jar Jar Binks

Disney again joined real and cartoon worlds in *Mary Poppins*. In this 1964 musical, Julie Andrews is the

Gollum's movements in *Lord of the Rings* are based on those of a real actor — Andy Serkis.

famous flying nanny. Disney weaves a magical web of animation around her. For example, when she gets tea in a real cafe, her waiters are four cartoon penguins.

How did Disney do it? When the live scenes were shot, the actors played their parts alongside cardboard cutouts. Studio artists drew in the cartoon characters later on.

Who Framed Roger Rabbit broke down all the barriers between people and cartoon figures. This 1988 film is a comedy, a thriller, and a murder mystery all rolled into one. Plus, real people and new cartoon creatures

Behind the Scenes:
The Making of Gollum

In *Lord of the Rings*, Gollum is a special effect. But all his movements are based on those of a real actor — Andy Serkis. The method used to make Gollum is called motion-capture animation.

Serkis did each scene wearing a costume covered with sensors. Each time he moved, the sensors sent data to a computer. When the scene ended, the computer had a complete record of his movements. At the same time, the filmmakers made a detailed model of Gollum. The model showed all of Gollum's muscles and bones. This model of Gollum was scanned into the computer. The computer then added the data from Serkis to the data about Gollum. The result is the figure you see on-screen. It moves and sounds like Serkis but looks like Gollum.

Director Peter Jackson used the same method in making *King Kong*. The same actor who "played" the skinny Gollum also played the giant ape!

CELEBRITY SNAPSHOT

George Lucas

Born: May 14, 1944, in Modesto, California

Film Career: Director, producer, writer

Academy Awards: Nominated for directing and writing *American Graffiti* (1973) and *Star Wars* (1977); received special award as producer (1991)

Top Films: : *Star Wars — Episode III: Revenge of the Sith*

Backstory: Yoda first appeared in *The Empire Strikes Back.* In that 1980 film, Yoda was a puppet, created and voiced by Frank Oz. Lucas hoped to make Yoda a digital character in *Phantom Menace.* But his team was unable to make the animated Yoda look real. For close-up scenes, they used a puppet instead. In *Star Wars: Episode II — Attack of the Clones,* Lucas finally was able to create an all-digital Yoda.

In recent *Star Wars* films, George Lucas (center) mixes real actors with animated characters.

The most recent *Star Wars* film used advanced computer animation methods to create this digital Yoda.

mingle with classic cartoon characters. Mickey Mouse and Donald Duck show up in Toontown. So do Bugs Bunny, Woody Woodpecker, and a true old-timer, Betty Boop.

Today, fantasy and science fiction films often include animated characters. For example, in *Star Wars: Episode I — The Phantom Menace*, the digital Jar Jar Binks had a major role. The animation worked. But many *Star Wars* fans hated the character. (Someone even wrote a song called "Jar Jar Binks Must Die!") Fans were much happier with the Yoda made by computer in the next *Star Wars* movie.

CHAPTER 5

New Styles, New Challenges

Cartoon makers are always looking for new worlds to capture. *The Lion King* and *Madagascar* are set in Africa. *Antz* and *A Bug's Life* take a comic look at the insect world.

Two recent films have undersea settings: *The SpongeBob SquarePants Movie* and *Finding Nemo*. Their styles couldn't be more different. *SpongeBob* is goofy fun. The hand-drawn animation is simple and low-tech. It makes no effort to look real. *Finding Nemo*, on the other hand, shows Pixar's high-tech approach. Computers make each fish beautifully. The fins glisten. The water shimmers. The film has many funny moments. But the story deals with a very serious subject — the death of a parent.

Cartoons with an Attitude

Some animators go for art. Others go for attitude. No

cartoon on TV or in the movies has more attitude than *South Park*. Trey Parker and Matt Stone made the movie *South Park: Bigger, Longer & Uncut* in 1999.

Behind the Scenes:
Crossing the Ocean

Artists in Asia work on many of the cartoons that air on American TV. For example, studios in South Korea have worked on *SpongeBob* and *The Powerpuff Girls*. South Korean artists also do much of the drawing for *The Simpsons*.

Parker created the *South Park* characters using cutouts made from construction paper. The animation style is crude. The language is even cruder. Parker and Stone made another movie in 2004 — *Team America: World Police*. This animated film was created with puppets.

Anime

Another cartoon trend comes from Japan. *Anime* (ah-nuh-MAY) is the Japanese word for animation. Some anime films are fine for young children. Other anime works are very violent. These films are meant for older viewers.

Today, the master of hand-drawn anime is Hayao Miyazaki. He began by drawing some of the classics of Japanese animation. His full-length film *Princess Mononoke* was a huge hit in Japan. So were *Spirited Away* and *Howl's*

CELEBRITY SNAPSHOT

Hayao Miyazaki

Born: January 5, 1941, in Tokyo, Japan

Film Career: Animator, director, producer, writer

Academy Awards: Best full-length animated film for *Spirited Away* (2002)

Other Top Films: : *My Neighbor Totoro; Kiki's Delivery Service; Princess Mononoke; Howl's Moving Castle*

Backstory: Most of the images in Miyazaki's films are drawn and painted by hand. He orders his aides to limit their use of computers. He says their job is "not to be accurate, not to be true. We're making a mystery here, so make it mysterious."

Animator Hayao Miyazaki also draws manga, a type of comic.

A young girl enters a scary world of witches, ghosts, and demons in Miyazaki's *Spirited Away*.

Moving Castle. English-language versions of these films have become popular in the United States.

Miyazaki's stories and artwork draw on Japanese folklore. Nature has tremendous power in his films. Spirits and demons dwell in the forests and mountains. His movies show how people need to make peace with each other and with the land.

His work has inspired many other artists — including Pixar's John Lasseter. "When we at Pixar feel that we're beating our heads against the wall," Lasseter says, "we . . . watch one of his films. It's like, whoa, look what he did. It's inspiration to power through that brick wall."

Glossary

Academy Award — also called an Oscar; an award given out by the movie industry.

backstory — the background story to something seen on screen.

dialogue — in a screenplay, the words the characters say to each other.

digital — created by computer.

director — the person who controls the creative part of making a movie.

frame — the separate photographs that make up a movie; also, the boundary that separates what can be seen on screen from what cannot.

nanny — someone who gets paid to take care of other people's children in the children's own home.

nominated — named or suggested as a candidate for a particular honor or position.

producer — the person who handles the business part of making a movie.

sensors — devices that receive and send data about the physical world.

soundtrack — the part of the movie film on which sound is recorded; the dialogue, music, and sound effects that accompany a film.

To Find Out More

Books

Backstage at an Animated Series. High Interest Books:
   Backstage Pass (series). Danny Fingeroth
   (Children's Press)

Christopher Hart's Animation Studio. Christopher Hart
   (Watson-Guptill Publications)

Computer Animator. Exploring Careers (series).
   Peggy J. Parks (KidHaven Press)

Computer Graphics & Animation. Computer Guides
   (series). Asha Kalbag (E.D.C. Publishing)

Videos

Monsters, Inc. (Disney/Pixar) G

Spirited Away (Walt Disney Video) PG

Who Framed Roger Rabbit (Disney Home Video) PG

Web Sites

Aardman Animations Ltd
www.aardman.com
A delightful site with links to Wallace & Gromit

Pixar Animation Studios
www.pixar.com
Pixar's official site; check out the link "How We Do It."

Publisher's note to educators and parents: Our editors have carefully reviewed
these Web sites to ensure that they are suitable for children. Many Web sites change
frequently, however, and we cannot guarantee that a site's future contents will
continue to meet our high standards of quality and educational value. Be advised
that children should be closely supervised whenever they access the Internet.

Index

About the Author

Geoffrey M. Horn has been a fan of music, movies, and sports for as long as he can remember. He has written more than three dozen books for young people and adults, along with hundreds of articles for encyclopedias and other works. He lives in southwestern Virginia, in the foothills of the Blue Ridge Mountains, with his wife, their collie, and four cats. A Mac computer user for more than twenty years, he dedicates this book to the creative spirits at Apple Computer and Pixar Animation Studios.